One Bipolar Family

One Family's Experience with Bipolar Illness: from Affliction toward Recovery

From Affliction toward Recovery

This is the true story of our family, all members being afflicted with Bipolar illness. Our journey is chronicled from the onset of the illness to the elusiveness of recovery.

We welcome you to delve into our world and come away with a better understanding of the affliction that is Bipolar illness and the desperate grasp we have made at recovery.

Dedication:

To Dr. Laura Lai, Glendora, CA
An excellent psychiatrist
A trusted friend

To Jan Dils
A wonderful counselor

A very special thank you to all family and friends who have stood by us in our darkest hours and rejoiced with us in our steps toward recovery.

Contents

Chapter 1

Mom

My Bipolar illness doesn't define me.

I am a mid- fifties woman, wife and mother of one. I am patient, loving, kind and tend to see the brighter side of life.

If you ask others what color I remind them of, they will describe me as the color yellow, bright and cheery.

I love to help others, especially my family. I am fiercely loyal. And I am fiercely determined to continue on my road to recovery.

I love to travel. I particularly love the ocean destinations. I've been to Tahiti, to the Caribbean and the Hawaiian islands several times.

In spite of all the pain and dysfunction this illness has caused I've been blessed to have been to some of my favorite places on earth with my family.

Genetics

I believe the onset of my illness began at conception. I believe the illness is at least partially a by-product of my dad's diagnosed paranoid schizophrenia.

My dad was hospitalized twice. He refused medication. Instead, he opted for electric shock treatments that produced short term memory loss. He drank copious amounts of alcohol to cope with his symptoms.

Looking back and having gone through what I have, I now realize my dad was a superman, holding down an insurance agent's job while dealing with his mental health issues. I can't say enough about his courage and fortitude.

On my mom's side, my maternal aunt committed suicide when she was in her twenties. My maternal uncle developed depression at 75 years old.

Stressful events in my childhood were caused by my dad's illness and his alcoholism. I lived in fear from the time I was six years old through my teens. Fear that my father would harm my mother, not me, was a constant stress.

I am the youngest in the birth order. My mom had me when she was 43. My dad was 46. Maybe the birth order and age of my parents when I was conceived were other factors that tended to predispose me toward this illness.

I believe all components were at the very least factors in my experience in becoming Bipolar.

I have three sisters, two with intermittent chemical dependency. One has no addictions. None of them are on psychiatric medication. None of them has been hospitalized due to their mental health.

I don't know how this illness managed to skip over them and hit me so hard. However, I wouldn't wish this illness on any of them.

They have been a steadfast source of comfort and support during my process toward recovery.

In the Workplace

Am I a productive person in the workplace in spite of this illness? Yes and no.

I can't seem to hold down a 9 to 5 job, mainly because I feel the traditional jobs are too taxing. The 9 to 5, 5 days a week schedule exhausts me.

My husband and I have our own company now. I work very well with him. Our temperaments jive. I also have a very flexible schedule. This is key in my ability to perform my functions for the company.

In my earlier years I obtained an International Marketing degree and worked several corporate temporary jobs. But then as my illness took on a life of its own, I found it harder and harder to stay focused. I wanted temporary jobs that were shorter and shorter in duration.

A Brewing Storm

Simultaneously, I became more and more drawn to my daughter. I wanted her to experience the different aspects of life.

From learning to play tennis, soccer, and swimming to taking after school shopping trips to the mall, day trips to Santa Barbara, and lunches at the beach, I wanted to be close to her.

I had this feeling that I was running out of time. I had to get it all in with her because I felt that I was going to just float away. I wouldn't be there to take care of her.

My fear was not unwarranted.

The Experience

Looking back, I sensed something was wrong the day my daughter was born. I couldn't make a connection with her. She was beautiful. But all I could feel was emptiness.

I knew something wasn't right. My husband stepped in to care for her, even waking up in the middle of the night to feed and change her.

We moved in with my husband's parents to get help. As time went on, what was determined to be postpartum stayed with me longer than usual. I wasn't functioning on all levels so we decided to continue living with his parents and I continued to experience mood swings.

I found some relief in running; running up hills, running at the park. I ran 5ks. I ran half-marathons. I ran until the endorphins couldn't do their job anymore on my moods. And then I crashed.

My daughter was 12. My husband was enmeshed in his work. They were taken by surprise when I started walking in the backyard muttering that I didn't know if I was in hell or on earth.

This was my first psychotic break.

Institutionalized

I have been in a mental facility four times. The first stay was confusing. I was being pumped with drugs, seeing a psychiatrist daily, and being told I was always going to be sick. I didn't get the right medication combination so I didn't exit very healthy.

I was shooting in the dark from that point on.

The subsequent hospital stays were interspersed with new psychiatrists who proved ineffectual until I met my current psychiatrist.

She is fantastic. She knows her stuff. She's caring and she really listens. I believe she has found the magic elixir of meds to see me through toward recovery.

Coping Day to Day

I am diagnosed Bipolar I. This means I have had at least one manic episode.

Currently, my moods are pretty stable. I get up feeling good and usually maintain this good feeling throughout the day. I'll have occasional blips, but they're not debilitating.

Before I got the right combination of medications, I couldn't rely on the day. I'd wake up very cautiously. How I felt in the morning set the tone for the day.

A big item for me with this illness is not to allow the psychosis to take hold. I'm basically useless if that happens.

The good thing is I haven't had a psychotic break in more than 5 years. As a result, today I consider myself highly functioning.

The only thing I really miss is being able to cry. Yes, *cry*. The medications I take do such a good job of making me stable and even tempered that I don't go low enough to cry. I'm happy the majority of the time, which is a good thing!

Also, holidays come and go. Sure I know it's Christmas, Easter, New Years, but my depth of feeling isn't there. A little like being on autopilot. It's a trade-off.

Triggers

Now that I've received treatment, there are still triggers that predispose me toward mania.

Coffee is one trigger. I know it's the caffeine. I started drinking coffee because my meds would make me so sleepy in the morning even though I take all my pills at night.

When I graduated to espresso, I started going borderline manic, buying any make-up I found appealing in the store. I tended to want to buy as many brands as I could afford that week - many colors, many brands. I spent over $4,000 in 6 months on cheap and sometimes not so cheap make-up.

I finally saw the correlation between coffee and mania when I switched to Green Tea. As soon as I made the switch, my purchases dropped to maybe one purchase a week. My doctor explained that the caffeine raises the dopamine levels in the brain, something I was trying to lower with my antipsychotic medication.

With all that caffeine I had been ingesting I was upping my Lithium Carbonate, adding 1 more to my daily maintenance dose, otherwise I couldn't sleep. With the switch to Green Tea my sleep improved and I was able to lower my Lithium back down to my maintenance dose.

Stress has the ability to also bring on a short term manic attack. I don't get depressed when I'm stressed. I get hyper-organized, racy, and I spend. If the stress goes unchecked and I become manic, I am vulnerable to a psychotic break.

Finally, substance abuse has played a role in my illness. I drink Charles Shaw which to me is a very weak wine. I drink everyday or every other day.

My doctor says that drinking more than one *small* glass of wine a day diminishes the potency of my medication. I have seen this. If I have more than one glass, I can't sleep as well. Also, I've noticed that I go a little manic. I start to buy makeup again. That's my clue that I have to pull back from my drinking.

Sometimes I drink for social reasons, sometimes when I'm under stress and sometimes when I just want to relax and listen to music and unwind. But for whatever reason, too much definitely throws me off kilter.

Counseling

I think counseling is helpful. I was lucky to get a good counselor who is very skilled, has a lot of experience, and is very knowledgeable because of her education and maturity.

My husband and I benefited from counseling because it helped us to heal from the damage our illnesses had done to our marriage.

13

During counseling, I didn't have to forgive my daughter, just my husband. Forgiveness came hard at first for me. My husband did a lot of damage. But as time passed, and I came to understand the Bipolar illness, I didn't judge him so harshly.

With medication and counseling my husband returned to the man I had fallen in love with so it was hard to hold a grudge. We've been able to move forward together.

Occasionally, I also had separate counseling when I was having problems due to medication adjustments or if I had a difficulty unrelated to my marriage.

One topic that has provided controversy is whether medication is absolutely necessary in treating Bipolar illness or if counseling can root out its cause.

I believe, through experience, that if I didn't have medication first the counseling would have proven futile.

Family

Love, support, and forgiveness have held our family together. I love my husband and daughter very much. The love has always been there, even when circumstances brought on by the illness were present.

I know this illness very well by now and I support my family by being available for them. I know when one of us is going down; I know when one of us is bordering on mania. I know when to support and when to back off;

when to let them go through what they have to go through.

We, as a family, are drawn to the ocean. It is our common point of relief, hope and struggle.

All of our vacations have involved ocean travel. The beauty, the symbolism, the refreshment are conducive to letting go and just being ourselves.

The struggle comes when one of us at one time or another during this illness has been internally dead to the beauty before us.

So in essence the ocean really symbolizes the ebb and flow of our Bipolar experience.

Medications

My medications include: 1) Zyprexa which is an antipsychotic 2) Clonazepam a sedative and anti-seizure 3) Effexor XR an antidepressant and finally 4) Lithium Carbonate. I have a target date set with my doctor to get off the Zyprexa so I can lose my extra weight.

It's really hard to deal with the weight gain inherent in some of the drugs I'm on. The combination of meds, particularly Zyprexa, has me weighing 100 pounds over my normal weight. I have tried to get off the Zyprexa, but each time I try I feel very scared and eventually I can't function.

I feel too good mentally to let go of the Zyprexa right now. But, my doctor has encouraged me to keep trying in my efforts to drop the Zyprexa. The weight is unhealthy and could cause more problems in the future.

Besides the weight gain, one of the side effects I have from my medication is a psoriatic condition on my hands, elbows and my feet. I have to put a cortisone cream on my hands nightly.

And finally, I have water retention if I take extra Lithium.

Chapter 2

Dad

I am more than Bipolar. I am an entrepreneur with a strong work ethic. I am resourceful. I am driven to always find a way to achieve my goals.

I have a love of the good life that permeates all aspects of my life.

I give freely to my family and those business associates that I respect.

My family always comes first now that I know how easily it can be threatened.

I can be the darkest hue of black when challenged and I can be the lighter shade of crimson when I am spending time with my family.

I am loving, jovial and kind.

Genetics

As a child, I was exposed to traumatic events, suffering a broken arm by my dad when I brought home too much candy.

My dad was Bipolar. So were my cousins and two uncles. They all disappeared in their thirties; just took off.

Initially, my dad was the exception. He stayed with the family during his minor breakdowns. But then in his fifties he had a major episode and disappeared in another country, just like his relatives. He returned to us 6 months later broke and disheveled.

He died of lymphoma after a 3 year battle with cancer.

Genetically I believe I am clearly predisposed toward Bipolar illness.

My extended family consists of a brother and sister. Neither is on psychiatric medication, nor are they diagnosed with Bipolar illness.

I don't understand the genetic process whereby they escaped Bipolar illness, but I'm extremely thankful for their good fortune.

In the Workplace

I've worked during my entire battle with Bipolar illness. I was the only one to really support the family.

My wife had severe postpartum so we were faced with a major obstacle at the onset of our life together.

She was unable to maintain three subsequent pregnancies.

She was unable to hold down a full-time job.

These factors really affected me. I think this was the beginning of my downward spiral.

I had a high risk occupation representing Las Vegas that fueled the availability of women, gambling, and the party scene for a large portion of my thirties and forties.

I finally cracked in my late forties. Not unlike my father, I took off to a foreign country and came back exhausted and broke.

I was very fortunate to get on my feet again and to resume making a living to support my family.

The Experience

As an adult, I knew something was wrong when I started having periods of extreme fatigue. I just wanted to stay in bed. I didn't want to shave because shaving to me meant that I was attempting to complete the day doing something, anything. The day frightened me.

Then after a few months of just hanging on, the switch flipped. I was full of exuberant energy. No business deal seemed unreasonable. No experience to be denied.

This flip flop between depression and mania would exist during a 20 year period. As I got older the periods of mania and depression got closer.

As my wife began to recover she began guiding me on my road to recovery, guiding me to great care as she received it. Thankfully, I was not subjected to a mental facility.

The Diagnosis

My diagnosis is Bipolar I. I have experienced at least one manic episode.

A typical day finds me waking up feeling pretty good, though some days are still a challenge.

If I wake up feeling the pit (a term I use to describe an actual feeling of heaviness and angst that radiates from my sternum), I can get through the day, but then I have to remember to take more Lithium Carbonate before bed. I'm usually good in a couple of days.

My cognition has been affected by the illness and the daily medication I have to take. Sometimes I lose my sense of physical direction. I'll be driving and have to pull over and get my bearings with my ipad. Thank goodness for technology!

Substance abuse hasn't played a role in my illness. I was never into drugs and I can drink one glass of wine with dinner and be done. At most, I drink 1-2 glasses of wine when I'm home watching T.V., maybe once a month.

Triggers

Now that I've received treatment I still experience triggers for my mania. Stress, lack of sleep and caffeine are the culprits.

Being the sole breadwinner, the bills fall on my shoulders and cause a lot of stress. When I'm able to produce a substantial income, I'm ok.

I need a consistent 8 hours of sleep each night. If I get overly stressed I need to go to sleep in the middle of the day. This will be followed by an extra Lithium capsule each night until I'm not sleeping midday. The cause, effect and treatment are pretty predictable.

Caffeine will wire me up. I don't drink it frequently anymore. Like my wife, I've switched to Green Tea.

Stress also brings out my mania in the form of online purchases. As the medication has taken hold I don't buy as much as I used to. Watches were my favorite purchase. I have a drawerful.

Counseling

Counseling was a great help for my wife and I. We both damaged the marriage. We were both untreated Bipolar people.

I think I was initially reacting to my wife's out of control mood swings. We fought all the time. Then I spun out of control becoming distant, unfaithful and angry.

When we finally got the right medications and were in sync, my wife started the counseling first and I followed. It really helped us work through all the hurt we'd caused each other.

After two years of counseling, we now see the counselor just once a month for maintenance.

<u>Family</u>

One word, one thought, one meaning being love has held our family together. I love my wife. We have a connection and a strong bond that was tested in the mania(s).

The connection triumphed and so did the bond. We have a compatibility that you only find between best friends.

I love my daughter. She is pulling up the rear with this illness. I've been heartbroken to see her go through what my wife and I have gone through. But I have hope that she is nearing the end of her medication journey and will finally find inner peace.

On our website is a beautiful picture of the ocean. It represents calm, peacefulness, family and regret.

Calm and peacefulness I have always felt when I look at a beautiful ocean picture. It reminds me of our family vacations, some better than others.

For example, I took my wife to Hawaii when she had her first manic episode. I didn't know what was going on with her. She was psychotic and very agitated. I took her to the Kea Lani Resort in Maui thinking that if she could get to her favorite place, she'd snap out of it. Back then I hadn't even heard of the term Bipolar.

She ended up staying in the room most of the time making telephone calls to our parish priest. She had sought him out before our trip desperately looking for an explanation as to what she was going through.

While in Maui, she made $800 in phone calls to him. At that point, I knew my plan wasn't working.

Years later, I can sincerely say that I can look at the ocean and remember the good times we've had, *emphasize* the good times, and downplay the bad times.

Medications

My medication regimen is: 1) Trileptal an anti-seizure medication 2) Lithium Carbonate a mood stabilizer 3) Ambien and Melatonin for sleep.

I'm fortunate to have not gained too much weight while on my medications. A bonus for me is that Lithium can cause weight loss in men. Unfortunately, for my wife and daughter, just the opposite effect in women, weight gain.

I've been lucky to not have severe side effects from my medications. But, I do have Psoriasis which is exacerbated by Lithium Carbonate.

I've also noticed slight short term memory loss. I leave the den to get something in the bedroom and come back empty handed, not remembering what I was looking for.

Ironically, and at the same time, I can reminisce about my deceased father when I was 5 years old showing me that my long term memory is still intact.

Chapter 3

Daughter

I define myself as a Gemini. I am the twin.

I love flamboyance in fashion. At the same time I am a mellow and gentle partner. I love and am kind to animals.

Pink is my favorite color and it represents the soft, feminine side of me. Totally opposite of the person I've been in the throes of the Bipolar illness.

I am on the road to maturity but I know that it is a road I sometimes resist.

I've had a chunk of my development as a person detoured due to my mania and depression. I still depend on others to help me with daily life.

My mom is my best friend. She knows Bipolar illness so well. She has travelled this path before me and I rely on her guidance.

I am grateful for all the help I receive from my mom, my dad, other family members and my doctor.

Genetics

Genetically, I think my mom and dad predisposed me towards Bipolar illness so that would make the onset of my illness at birth.

I also experienced a lot of trauma as a child because my parents were both sick.

I never had physical abuse. I had emotional trauma. The emotional trauma wasn't intentional, but it was constantly there. I witnessed a lot of fights when my parents interacted.

I believe this environment and my inherited genes are the factors that made me Bipolar.

Substance Abuse and the Experience

I first suspected I was sick when I started feeling and acting strangely.

I was usually quiet, more reserved when I was growing up. Then I started having really bad mood swings and acting out when I was living with my boyfriend in Las Vegas.

I was 24. I used to frequent the nightclubs in my mania. That's when I came across recreational drugs and became addicted to Methamphetamines.

It destroyed my relationship with my boyfriend.

It also destroyed my already compromised health. My teeth alone are a mess from the Meth. I've racked up a $13,000 bill with the dentist.

I used to use Meth for weight loss.

I know the Meth didn't help my Bipolar illness. It made it infinitely worse. If I took drugs (Meth) and a lot of alcohol now, that would fuel a mania.

I also have to stay away from Marijuana. It exacerbates my symptoms.

Under the influence, I used to shop online obsessively for clothes and jewelry. I was always on Facebook. I also wanted to party all the time, going out to nightclubs, meeting guys, drinking and smoking.

At 32, I finally stopped the drug use. I'm clean now and I'm being treated for Bipolar illness. My daily pill container is the constant reminder of my past and present struggle.

With the exception of contemplating a pregnancy, getting off my medication is not an option.

Now, alcohol by itself in moderation doesn't make me manic. I use alcohol to buffer the hard parts of the day.

I drink Wild Turkey; a sip here, a sip there. Just to take the edge off. This of course is against doctor's orders. I used to carry a flask around with me all the time. Since the introduction of Cymbalta, an antidepressant, my desire to drink is somewhat less.

Even though I've stopped all recreational drugs, I still don't have it all together. I suffer throughout the day. I have mood swings. I struggle to get out of bed most mornings and when I do I don't feel good.

I feel low and I can't think clearly. I have panic attacks daily. Sleep is my only true peace.

At family gatherings I sometimes stand in the background, or stay in my room and watch television. Rarely, being social overrides my inability to be completely present.

Fortunately, my psychiatrist found a combination of medications that makes me feel a little better.

I have to hang on to hope amidst the difficulty.

Psychoses and Diagnosis

I have been diagnosed Bipolar I. I had a short psychotic break before medication.

I awoke from a dream and thought I was in a foxhole! I started calling friends in a panic telling them I didn't know where I was.

Needless to say I lost some friends through this experience. They couldn't figure out what had happened to me.

My mom got me into the doctor that week. I was diagnosed Bipolar I and treatment commenced.

I'm the same age my mom was when she had her first hospital stay for her psychotic break. Even though I've never been in a mental hospital, there have been days when I felt I needed to go. I'm scared, but I think I'm going to dodge that bullet. I have a great psychiatrist and supportive parents.

Ultimately, after seeing what my mom and dad have been through, I'm convinced that arriving at the right combination of medications is the key to my recovery.

I'm getting close to that point. Medications take time to work. I won't know if this combo is a good fit for me for a few more weeks.

Barring any downturn in my illness, I still make plans for a future. I have tentative plans to start cosmetology school sometime this year.

My Support

My mom has held us together as a family. My dad paid the bills, which is *huge*, and which I know enabled my mom to help my dad and I.

My mom has been there emotionally and physically to support us through this illness. She's guided us through the maze that is the Bipolar experience.

My mom got my dad and I to the right doctor.

We've avoided institutionalization because of her guidance.

My mom has a lot more battle scars from this illness than my dad and I, but she doesn't complain. She's too busy helping us, making sure we're o.k., adhering to the path toward recovery.

Counseling

Unfortunately, counseling didn't help me at all.

I saw several counselors before I gave up. I just couldn't connect with the counselors. I couldn't connect with the counseling process. Maybe if I kept going, looking, I would have found someone.

Talking to my mom really is a form of counseling for me. She knows everything I've been through in mania and depression. She doesn't judge me because she knows how completely ruthless this illness can be. It causes you to do things you normally wouldn't do. To hurt people you wouldn't think of hurting.

One other point is that I am not chemically balanced. When that happens, maybe then I can try to integrate the counseling process into my recovery.

Family

The ocean has significance in a mixed way for my family. I see the ocean and our vacations as an ultimate attempt to be together, to bond.

But, it also reminds me of the times I've been on vacation with my parents, and because I wasn't on the right meds, I couldn't really enjoy myself.

I would look at the ocean and I would feel hollow, no depth of feeling. It was an agonizing experience.

My mom and dad would reassure me it was going to get better. They knew because they had gone through the exact experience at one time or another before they became chemically balanced.

Medications

My medications include: 1) Cymbalta an antidepressant 2) Geodon an antipsychotic 3) Clonazepam for anxiety and seizures 4) Ambien for sleep and 5) Lithium Carbonate for mood. Cymbalta was recently added to my regimen and I feel a little better.

Side effects from my medication, besides weight gain, are few. Like my dad, I have psoriasis. Fortunately, I only have it on my scalp. If I take extra Lithium I notice a flare-up of patches on my scalp.

Finally, I grew up with an eating disorder. I'm leery of anything (i.e. medication) I consume. Mentally, it is so hard when I gain just one pound. I desperately want to feel good. Weight wise, I just wish the price wasn't so high for me.

Conclusion

In the storm that is Bipolar illness, we are not all quite out on the other side. Our daughter is still in the storm.

I've been told you're never cured of your Bipolar illness, but varying degrees of recovery are definitely possible.

I know it's possible because my husband and I have experienced respites from the turbulence that is Bipolar illness. We have come out far enough on the other side to enjoy and love each other and connect with our extended family.

Our hope now is for our daughter's recovery. We pray that her days become brighter and that Bipolar illness becomes nothing more than a manageable nuisance.

If you see yourself in our stories, please don't hesitate to get help. It is a process that begins with one step and continues until you can see the light on the horizon.

Resources

Recommended Reading:
http://en.wikipedia.org/wiki/Bipolardisorder

Coping & Support Resources for Bipolar Disorder
*http://bipolar.about.com/od/support/Coping_Support_*
Resources_for_Bipolar_Disorder.htm

www.OneBipolarFamily.com

Notes

www.ingramcontent.com/pod-product-compliance
Lightning Source LLC
Chambersburg PA
CBHW060015300526
45794CB00003B/1193